FOR THE LOVE OF CATS

A Collection of Drawings by Lewis McClellan
With Writings Chosen by John Gill

The Crossing Press
Trumansburg, NY 14886

To Claudia

Cover and Book Design by Betsy Bayley
Typesetting by Martha Jean Waters

Printed in the U.S.A.

Library of Congress Cataloging-in-Publication Data

McClellan, Lewis,
For the love of cats.

1. McClellan, Lewis. 2. Cats in art. 3. Cats in literature. I. Gill, John, 1924- . II. title.
NC139.M34A4 1985 741.973 85-17431
ISBN 0-89594-185-6

ISBN 0-89594-174-0 paper

ACKNOWLEDGMENTS

The Bodley Head Ltd.: "Diamond Cut Diamond" from *Diamond Cut Diamond* by Ewart Milne, 1950.

Coward-McCann, Inc.: "Calling the Cat" from *Compass Rose* by Elizabeth Coatsworth, copyright © 1929 by Coward-McCann, Inc.

The Crossing Press: "Cat," and "The Cats In The Colosseum" from *The Cats In The Colosseum* by John Stevens Wade, copyright © 1972 by John Stevens Wade.

Doubleday and Co., Inc.: from "the song of mehitabel" from *Archy and Mehitabel* by Don Marquis, copyright © 1933 by Doubleday and Co., Inc.

Eleanor Farjeon: "Cats" copyright © 1960 by Eleanor Farjeon.

Farrar, Straus & Cudahy Inc.: "The Long-Cat" from *Creatures Great and Small* by Colette, copyright © 1904 by Colette Willy, trans. by Enid McLeod.

Farrar, Straus & Giroux, Inc.: "The Happy Cat" from *The Complete Poems* by Randall Jarrell, copyright © 1945 by Randall Jarrell.

Mary Gilliland: "Zorro" copyright © 1985 by Mary Gilliland.

Harcourt, Brace and Company: "106" from *Collected Poems* by e.e. cummings, copyright © 1938 by e.e. cummings.

Alfred A. Knopf, "Mr. Big" from *My Mother's Body* by Marge Piercy, copyright © 1985 by Marge Piercy.

David Bennett Laing: "Miao" from *The Collected Poems of Dilys Laing*, published by The Press of Case Western Reserve University, copyright © 1967 Estate of Dilys Laing by David Bennett Laing. By permission of Alexander Laing, Administrator of the Estate of Dilys Laing.

Little, Brown and Company: "The Cat" from *Many Long Years Ago* by Ogden Nash, copyright © 1933 by Ogden Nash.

Macmillan Publishing Co., Inc.: "The Mysterious Cat" from *Johnny Appleseed and Other Poems* by Vachel Lindsay, copyright © renewed 1942 by Elizabeth C. Lindsay in *Collected Poems*, Macmillan Publishing Co.

New Directions Books: "Moon Tiger" from *Relearning The Alphabet* by Denise Levertov, copyright © 1970 by Denise Levertov Goodman. "Nansen" from *The Back Country* by Gary Snyder, copyright © 1968 by Gary Snyder. "Poem" from *Collected Earlier Poems* by William Carlos Williams, copyright © 1938 by New Directions Publishing Corporation.

Random House, Inc. "Major is a fine cat" and "Nodding" from *Me Again, Uncollected Writings* by Stevie Smith, copyright © 1981 by James MacGibbon.

Charles Scribner's Sons: "Cat & The Weather" from *To Mix With Time,* New and Selected Poems by May Swenson, copyright © 1963 by May Swenson.

Simon & Schuster, Inc.: "A Cat" by John Gittings from *Miracles,* edited by Richard Lewis, copyright © 1966 by Richard Lewis, by permission of Simon & Schuster, Inc.

William Jay Smith: "Cat" from *Boy Blue's Book of Beasts,* copyright © 1957 by William Jay Smith.

Wesleyan University Press: "The Cat" from *The Complete Poems of W.H. Davies,* copyright © 1963 by Jonathan Cape, Ltd.

A Home Without A Cat

A home without a cat–and a well-fed, well-petted and properly revered cat–may be a perfect home, perhaps, but how can it prove its title?

Mark Twain

It is an amiable part of human nature, that we should love our animals; it is even better to love them to the point of folly, than not to love them at all.

Stevie Smith

The Friendship of A Cat

It is no easy task to win the friendship of a cat. He is a philosopher, sedate, tranquil, a creature of habit, a lover of decency and order. He does not bestow his regard lightly, and, though he may consent to be your companion, he will never be your slave. Even in his most affectionate moods he preserves his freedom, and refuses a servile obedience. But once gain his confidence, and he is a friend for life. He shares your hours of work, of solitude, of melancholy. He spends whole evenings on your knee, purring and dozing, content with your silence, and spurning for your sake the society of his kind.

Theophile Gautier

Take A Cat

Take a cat and feed him well with milk
And tender flesh and make his bed of silk
But let him see a mouse go by the wall–
Quickly he leaves milk and flesh and all
And every dainty that is in the house
Such appetite he has to eat a mouse.

Geoffrey Chaucer

Everyone is aware that a perfectly comfortable, well-fed cat will occasionally come to his house and settle there, deserting a family by whom it is lamented, and to whom it could, if it chose, find its way back with ease. This conduct is a mystery which may lead us to infer that cats form a great secret society, and that they come and go in pursuance of some policy connected with education, or perhaps with witchcraft.

Andrew Lang

Cat & The Weather

Cat takes a look at the weather:
snow;
puts a paw on the sill;
his perch is piled, is a pillow.

Shape of his pad appears:
will it dig? No,
not like sand,
like his fur almost.

But licked, not liked:
too cold.
Insects are flying, fainting down.
He'll try

to bat one against the pane.
They have no body and no buzz,
and now his feet are wet;
it's a puzzle.

Shakes each leg,
then shakes his skin
to get the white flies off;
looks for his tail,

tells it to come on in
by the radiator.
World's turned queer
somehow: all white,

no smell. Well, here
inside it's still familiar.
He'll go to sleep until
it puts itself right.

May Swenson

Having slept, the cat gets up,
And with great yawns,
Goes love-making

Issa

Poem

As the cat
climbed over
the top of

the jamcloset
first the right
forefoot

carefully
then the hind
stepped down

into the pit of
the empty
flowerpot.

William Carlos Williams

Under-The-Table-Manners

It's very hard to be polite
    If you're a cat.
When other folks are up at table
Eating all that they are able,
    You are down upon the mat
    If you're a cat

You're expected just to sit
    If you're a cat.
Not to let them know you're there
By scratching at the chair,
    Or a light, respected pat
    If you're a cat.

You are not to make a fuss
    If you're a cat.
Tho' there's fish upon the plate
You're expected just to wait,
    Wait politely on the mat
    If you're a cat.

Anon.

Sonnet To Mrs Reynolds' Cat

Cat, who has passed the grand climacteric,
How many mice and rats has in thy days
Destroyed? How many titbits stolen? Gaze
With those bright languid segments green, and prick
Those velvet ears–but prithee do not stick
Thy latent claws in me–and upraise
Thy gentle mew–and tell me all thy frays
Of fish and mice and rats and tender chicks.
Nay, look not down, nor lick thy dainty wrists.
For all the wheezy asthma, and for all
Thy tail's tip is nicked off, and though the fists
Of many a maid have given thee many a maul.
  Still is thy fur as when the lists
In youth thou enterd'st on glass-bottled wall.

John Keats

(Miao)*

I put down my book
The Meaning of Zen
and see the cat smiling
  into her fur
as she delicately combs it
  with her rough pink tongue.

"Cat, I would lend you this
  book to study
but it appears that you have
  already read it."

She looks up and gives me
  her full gaze.
"Don't be ridiculous," she purrs.
  "I wrote it."

Dilys Laing

**Miao*: Excellent, mysterious, subtle

Zorro

A crescent in April snow
marks the grave
where your body has lain
for a week.

You didn't keep yourself separate
the way cats should.
Half your curiosity
nosed out human ways.

The sky falls in white flakes
as your spirit flies
free of pain,
a wild bird.

You ate so many,
rabbit biter, bat catcher.
Remembering your fierce tenderness
we buried you with feathers.

Mary Gilliland

There was a wee bit mousikie,
   That lived in Bilberary-O,
It couldno' get a bite o'cheese,
   For Cheatie-Pussy-Catty-O.

It said unto the cheesity,
   "Oh fain would I be at ye-O
If 'Twere not' for the cruel claws
   O' Cheatie-Pussy-Catty-O."

Anon.

Stately, lordly friend,
        Condescend
Here to sit by me, and turn
Glorious eyes that smile and burn,
Golden eyes, love's lustrous meed,
On the golden page I read.

Algernon Charles Swinburne

Cornell

She sights a bird–she chuckles–
She flattens–then she crawls–
She runs without the look of feet–
Her eyes increase to Balls–

Her Jaws stir–twitching–hungry–
Her Teeth can hardly stand–
She leaps, but Robin leaped the first–
Ah, Pussy, of the Sand,

The Hopes so juicy ripening–
You almost bathed your Tongue–
When Bliss dissolved a hundred wings–
And fled with every one–

Emily Dickinson

Cats

Cats sleep
Anywhere,
Any table,
Any chair,
Top of piano,
Window-ledge,
In the middle,
On the edge,
Open drawer,
Empty shoe,
Anybody's
Lap will do,
Fitted in a
Cardboard box,
In the cupboard
With your frocks–
Anywhere!
They don't care!
Cats sleep
Anywhere

Eleanor Farjeon

From the dawn of creation the cat has known his place, and he has kept it, practically untamed and unspoiled by man. Of all animals, he alone attains to the Contemplative Life. He regards the wheel of existence from without, like the Buddha. There is no pretence of sympathy about the cat. He lives alone, aloft, sublime, in a wise passiveness.

Andrew Lang

The Mysterious Cat

I saw a proud, mysterious cat,
I saw a proud, mysterious cat,
Too proud to catch a mouse or rat–
Mew, mew, mew.

But catnip she would eat, and purr,
But catnip she would eat, and purr,
And goldfish she did much prefer–
Mew, mew, mew.

I saw a cat–'twas but a dream,
I saw a cat–'twas but a dream,
Who scorned the slave that brought her cream–
Mew, mew, mew.

Unless the slave were dressed in style,
Unless the slave were dressed in style,
And knelt before her all the while–
Mew, mew, mew.

Did you ever hear of a thing like that?
Did you ever hear of a thing like that?
Oh, what a proud, mysterious cat.
Oh, what a proud, mysterious cat.
Oh, what a proud, mysterious cat.
Mew . . . mew . . . mew.

Vachel Lindsay

Epitaph

Bathsheba:–
To whom none ever said scat.
No worthier cat
Ever sat on a mat
Or caught a rat:–
  Requies-cat.

John Greenleaf Whittier

The Cat

You get a wife, you get a house,
Eventually you get a mouse.
You get some words regarding mice,
You get a kitty in a trice.
By two A.M. or thereabout,
The mouse is in, the cat is out.
It dawns upon you, in your cot,
The mouse is silent, the cat is not.
Instead of Pussy, says your spouse,
You should have bought another mouse.

Ogden Nash

Nodding

Tizdal my beautiful cat
Lies on the old rag mat
In front of the kitchen fire.
Outside the night is black.

The great fat cat
Lies with his paws under him
His whiskers twitch in a dream,
He is slumbering.

The clock on the mantlepiece
Ticks unevenly, tic toc, tic-toc
Good heavens what is the matter
With the kitchen clock?

Outside an owl hunts,
Hee hee hee hee,
Hunting in the Old Park
From his snowy tree.
What on earth can he find in the park tonight,
It is so wintry?

Now the fire burns suddenly too hot
Tizdal gets up to move,
Why should such an animal
Provoke our love?

The twigs from the elder bush
Are tapping on the window pane
As the wind sets them tapping,
Now the tapping begins again.

One laughs on a night like this
In a room half firelight half dark
With a great lump of a cat
Moving on the hearth,
And the twigs tapping quick,
And the owl in an absolute fit
One laughs supposing creation
Pays for its long plodding
Simply by coming to this–
Cat, night, fire–and a girl nodding.

Stevie Smith

Pussy-cat ate the dumplings, the dumplings;
  Pussy-cat ate the dumplings.
Mamma stood by, and cried, "Oh, fie!"
  Why did you eat the dumplings?"

old ditty

Ptolemy

The limpid eyes, the curved walk, the way
he sits on my shoulder and burrows his head
into my neck, the tufts shafting delicately out
of his ears, the little feline skunk, black with white
paws and half white face, named Ptolemy.

He vanished out of my life one day, the legend (in
our heads) having it that he ventured into the
woods that morning, saw an animal who was new to
him, and, brave to the point of absolute folly,
went up to make friends with a fox.

Elaine Goldman Gill

Moon Tiger

The moon tiger.
In the room, here.
It came in, it is
prowling sleekly
under and over
the twin beds.
See its small head,
silver smooth,
hear the pad of its
large feet. Look,
its white stripes
in the light that slid
through the jalousies.
It is sniffing our
clothes, its cold nose
nudges our bodies.
The beds are narrow,
but I'm coming in with you.

Denise Levertov

Within that porch, across the way,
I see two naked eyes this night;
Two eyes that neither shut nor blink,
Searching my face with a green light.

But cats to me are strange, so strange–
I cannot sleep if one is near;
And though I'm sure I see those eyes,
I'm not so sure a body's there!

W.H. Davies

why did you go
little fourpaws?
you forgot to shut
your big eyes.

where did you go?
like little kittens
are all the leaves
which open in the rain.

little kittens who
are called spring,
is what we stroke
maybe asleep?

do you know? or maybe did
something go away
ever so quietly
when we weren't looking.

e.e. cummings

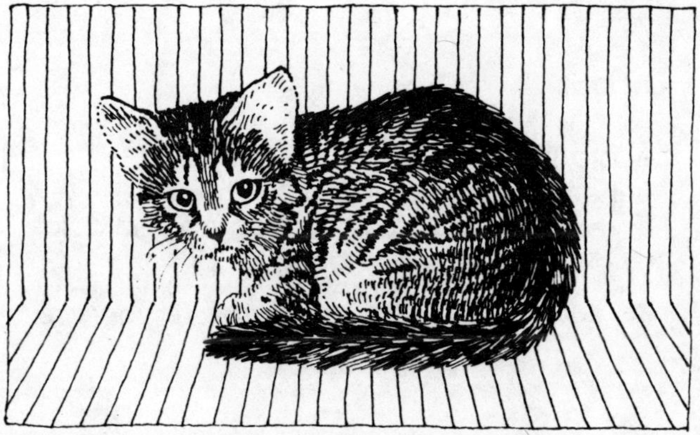

My Cat

My pretty cat to my heart I hold,
My heart ever warm to her;
Let me look in thine eyes of agate and gold;
Thy claws keep sheathed in fur.

Charles Baudelaire

Though the cat winks awhile, yet sure she is not blind.

English proverb

The old cat sits
on the back fence.
It's getting dark.
She'll wait a while
and then jump down.
She keeps so cool;
plays with her mouse.
Sometimes I think
she just pretends;
pretends a leaf
has fur and paws.
There's nothing bad
about that cat.
It's the design:
give a cat feet,
eyes, and a mind,
then watch it wait
and keep so cool.
I love that cat;
love those killer
paws, candle eyes.
It's getting dark.
Only an eye
of daylight squints
where the sun rolls.
She's ready now.
Bless, bless us all.

John Stevens Wade

Hey, my kitten, my kitten,
  Hey, my kitten, my deary;
Such a sweet pet as this
  Was neither far nor neary.

old ditty

When I play with my cat who knows whether I do not make her more sport than she makes me?

Michel de Montaigne

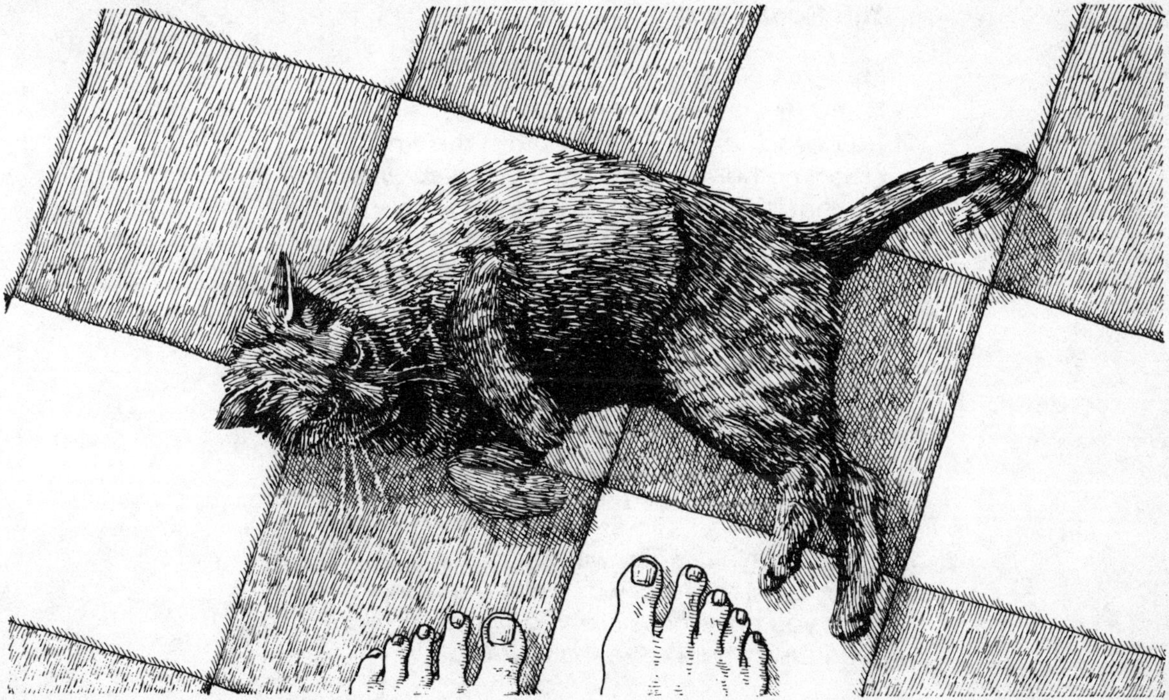

The Happy Cat

The cat's asleep; I whisper *kitten*
Till he stirs a little and begins to purr–
He doesn't wake. Today out on the limb
(The limb he thinks he can't climb down from)
He mewed until I heard him in the house.
I climbed up to get him down: he mewed.
What he says and what he sees are limited.
My own response is even more constricted.
I think, "It's lucky; what you have is too."
What do you have except–well, me?
I joke about it but it's not a joke:
The house and I are all he remembers.
Next month how will he guess that it is winter
And not just entropy, the universe
Plunging at last into its cold decline?
I cannot think of him without a pang.
Poor rumpled thing, why don't you see
That you have no more, really, than a man?
Men aren't happy: why are you?

Randall Jarrell

Marigold

She moved through the garden in glory, because
She had very long claws at the end of her paws.
Her back was arched, her tail was high,
A green fire glared in her vivid eye;
And all the Toms, though never so bold,
Quailed at the martial Marigold.

Richard Garnett

From **Last Words To A Dumb Friend**

Pet was never mourned as you,
Purrer of the spotless hue,
Plumy tail, and wistful gaze
While you humoured our queer ways,
Or outshrilled your morning call
Up the stairs and through the hall–
Foot suspended in its fall–
While, expectant you would stand
Arched, to meet the stroking hand;
Till your way you choose to wend
Yonder, to your tragic end.

Never another pet for me!
Let your place all vacant be;
Better blankness day by day
Than companion torn away.
Better bid his memory fade,
Better blot each mark he made,
Selfishly escape distress
By contrived forgetfulness,
Than preserve his prints to make
Every morn and eve an ache.

Thomas Hardy

Pangur Ban

I and Pangur Ban, my cat,
'Tis a like task we are at;
Hunting mice is his delight,
Hunting words I sit all night.

Oftentimes a mouse will stray
In the hero Pangur's way;
Oftentimes my keen thought set
Takes a meaning in its net.

When a mouse darts from its den,
Oh, how glad is Pangur then!
Oh, what gladness do I prove
When I solve the doubts I love!

So in peace our task we ply,
Pangur Ban–my cat–and I;
In our arts we find our bliss,
I have mine and he has his.

Irish monk, 9th century

Major is a fine cat
What is he at?
He hunts birds in the hydrangea
And in the tree
Major was ever a ranger
He ranges where no one can see.

Sometimes he goes up to the attic
With a hooped back
His paws hit the iron rungs
Of the ladder in a quick kick
How can this be done?
It is a knack.

Oh Major is a fine cat
He walks cleverly
And what is he at, my fine cat?
No one can see.

Stevie Smith

Her conscious tail her joy declared;
The fair round face, the snowy beard,
  The velvet of her paws,
Her coat, that with the tortoise vies,
Her ears of jet, and emerald eyes, . . .

Thomas Gray

Mimi

They no instrument use ever,
   Each is his own flute and viol;
All their noses trumpets are
   Bellies, drums, and no denial.

They in chorus raise their voices,
   In one general intermezzo,
Playing fugues, as if by Bach,
   Or by Guido of Arezzo.

Wild the symphonies they're singing,
   Like capriccios of Beethoven
Or by Berlioz, who's excelled
   By their strains so interwoven.

Heinrich Heine

Double Dutch

That crafty cat, a buff-black Siamese
Sniffing through wild wood, sagely, silently goes
Prick ears, lank legs, alertly twitching nose,
And on her secret errand reads with ease
A language no man knows.

Walter de la Mare

Calling The Cat

Now from the dark, a deeper dark,
The cat slides,
Furtive and aware,
His eyes still shine with meteor spark,
The cold dew weighs his hair.
Suspicious,
Hesitant, he comes,
Stepping morosely from the night,
Held but repelled,
Repelled but held
By lamp and firelight.

Now call your blandest,
Offer up
The sacrifice of meat,
And snare the wandering soul with greeds,
Give him to drink and eat,
And he shall walk fastidiously
Into the trap of old
On feet that still smell delicately
Of withered ferns and mould.

Elizabeth Coatsworth

Atossa, the Persian Cat

Thou has seen Atossa sage
Sit for hours beside thy cage;
Thou wouldst chirp, thou foolish bird,
Flutter, chirp,–she never stirred!
What were now these toys to her?
Down she sank amid her fur;
Eyed thee with a soul resign'd,
And thou deemedst cats were kind!
–Cruel, but composed and bland,
Dumb, inscrutable, and grand;
So Tiberius might have sat,
Had Tiberius been a cat.

Matthew Arnold

I found this wall a good place to study tomcats, not so much their habits as their ceremonial procedure, governed by a kind of choreography. Unlike the females, they are more noisy than warlike and they try to gain time by palavers. Hence all the snarling preambles. Not that they do not know how to fight cruelly once they come to grips; but as a rule they are far removed from the silent and furious grapplings of the females. The she-cat we had at the same time as the Long-cat literally flew into battle if a female ventured into her haunts. Barely touching the ground, she would pounce on the enemy, even if it were her own offspring. She fought as a bird does, going for her adversary's head. I never saw her chastise a male, except for a few cuffs, for as soon as the males saw her they fled, while she followed them with a look of inexpressible contempt.

Colette

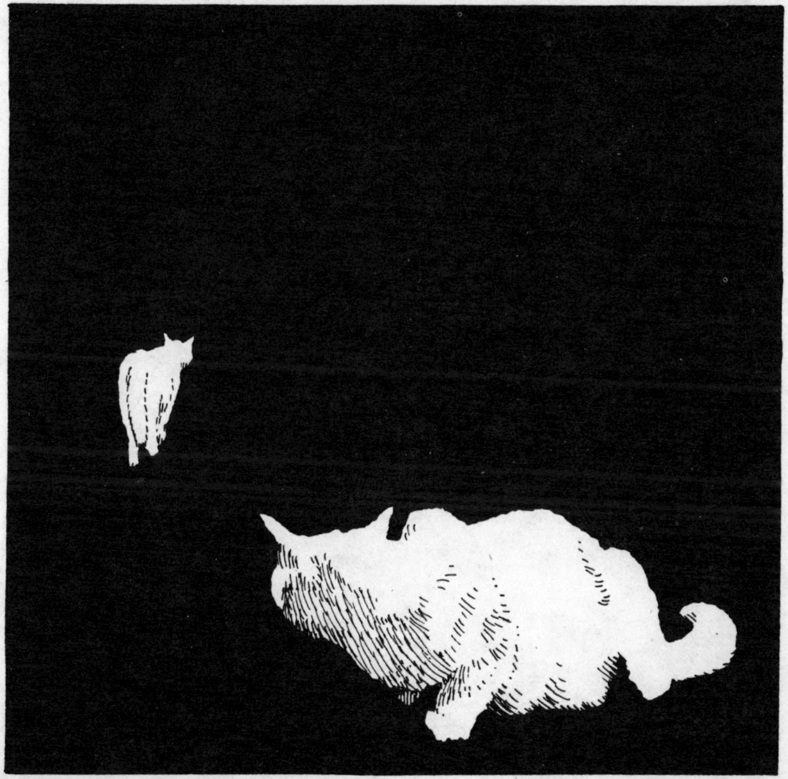

The day is young, said the cat, remembering that he could wait.

Russian proverb

Silently licking his gold-white paw
Oh gorgeous Celestino, for
God made lovely things, yet
Our lovely cat surpasses them all.
The gold, the iron, the waterfall,
The nut, the peach, apple, granite
Are lovely things to look at, yet,
Our lovely cat surpasses them all.

John Gittings

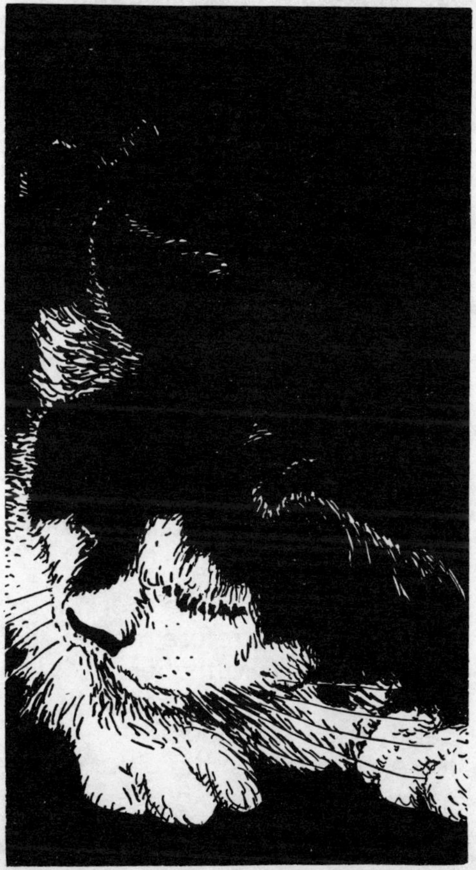

From **The Song of Mehitabel**

i wake the world from sleep
as i caper and sing and leap
when i sing my wild free tune
wotthehell wotthehell
under the blear eyed moon
i am pelted with cast off shoon
but wotthehell wotthehell

do you think that i would change
my present freedom to range
for a castle or moated grange
wotthehell wotthehell
cage me and i d go frantic
my life is so romantic
capricious and corybantic
and i m toujours gai toujours gai

i know that i am bound
for a journey down the sound
in the midst of a refuse mound
but wotthehell wotthehell
oh i should worry and fret
death and i will coquette
there s a dance in the old dame yet
toujours gai toujours gai

don marquis

The Retired Cat

A Poet's Cat, sedate and grave
As poet well could wish to have,
Was much addicted to inquire
For nooks to which she might retire,
And where, secure as mouse in chink,
She might repose, or sit and think.
I know not where she caught the trick;
Nature perhaps herself had cast her
In such a mold *philosophic,*
Or else she learned it of her master.
Sometimes ascending, debonair,
An apple tree or lofty pear,
Lodged with convenience in the fork,
She watched the gardener at his work;
Sometimes her ease and solace sought
In an old empty watering-pot,
There wanting nothing save a fan
To seem some nymph in her sedan,
Appareled in exactest sort,
And ready to be borne to court.

William Cowper

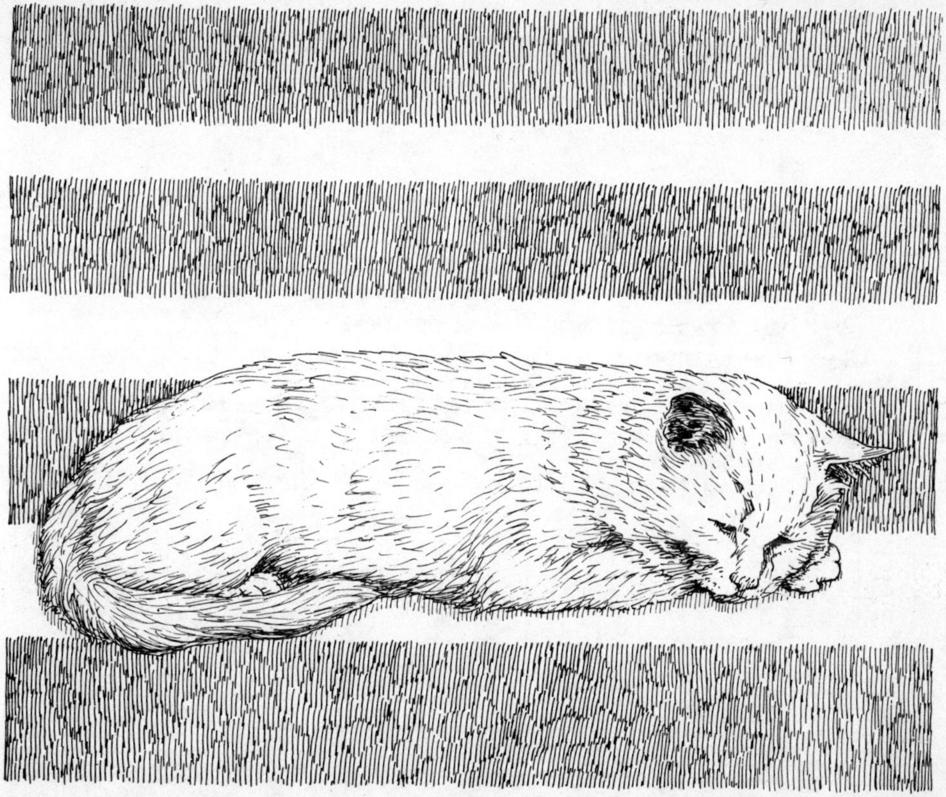

His tongue is sponge, and brush, and towel, and currycomb.
Well he knows what work it can be made to do,
Poor little wash-rag, smaller than my thumb.

His nose touches his back, touches his hind paws too.
Every patch of fur is raked, and scraped, and smoothed.

Hippolyte Taine

Nansen

I found you on a rainy morning
After a typhoon
In a bamboo grove at Daitoku-ji.
Tiny wet rag with a
Huge voice, you crawled under the fence
To my hand. Left to die.
I carried you home in my raincoat.
"Nansen, cheese!" you'd shout an answer
And come running.
But you never got big.
Bandy-legged bright little dwarf–
Sometimes not eating, often coughing
Mewing bitterly at inner twinge.

Now, thin and older, you won't eat
But milk and cheese. Sitting on a pole
In the sun. Hardy with resigned
Discontent.
You just weren't made right. I saved you,
And your three-year life has been full
Of mild, steady pain.

Gary Snyder

Reposed like the Sphinx in noble attitude,
In far lonely wastes of desert solitude,
They muse forever in an endless dream.

Charles Baudelaire

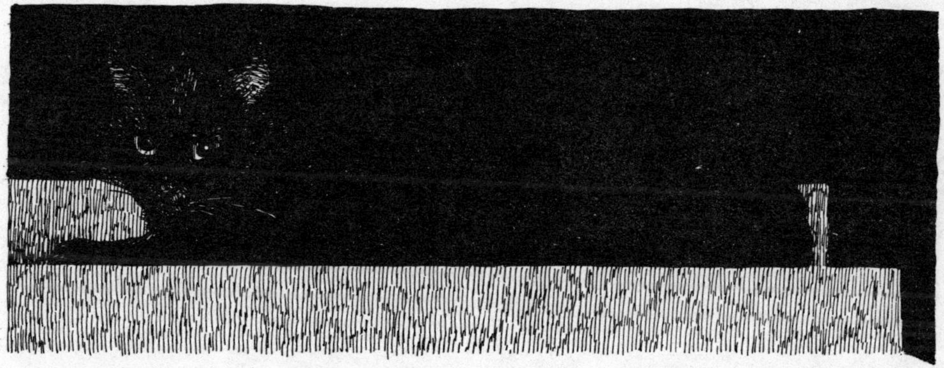

A cat I keep,
  That plays about my house,
Grown fat with eating
  Many a miching mouse

Robert Herrick

Mr. Big

Darkest chocolate, bittersweet,
the muscled power of horse's
haunches, the sleekness of a seal,
the swagger of a heavyweight
strolling to the ring:

Jim Beam works hard as overlord
hustling to rule his turf in winter
when only the great horned owl
can frighten him. But July Fourth
brings up the summer people

with their dogs, their cats,
their children, their dirt bikes,
their firecrackers. All summer
he collects scars and anger
trying to boss his ward.

He gets leaner, meaner.
He sulks and roars in baritone
O my unappreciated soul, all night.
He wants to be force-fed
love like chicken soup.

He wants love to chase him
like a panting dog,
without asking, without earning.
Jim Beam, you're indistinguishable
from half the men I've adored.

Being a cat you are lucky.
I do carry you off by force
and today you lie by the computer
on a satin pillow and eat turkey
and suffer, suffer your belly

to be scratched and endure
your chin chucked and tickled, at ease,
air conditioned while it's ninety out.
O Jim Beam, this must
be love: will you marry me?

Marge Piercy

1985

From **The Cats In The Colosseum**

I saw nine of them sleeping in the sun.
They were like dead gladiators from several nations:
One was a fierce African, he wore
a helmet of battered fur; two were
Asians, they had mysterious Eastern masks
strapped firmly to their faces with tiger stripes;
three were stout Persians, they were bundled in robes
of white, off-white, and grey; two were obviously
Barbarians, dingy but very strong;
one was delicate and slight, but his proud scars
were long and overlapping like twine.

One by one they rose from the crumbling pedestals
as a half-bowl splash of sunlight leaked
from the Colosseum and drenched the hills of Rome.
Late afternoon. Time for these gladiators
to rat where the lions roared centuries back.
I watched them go. The wind rose from the throats
of a hundred entrances and became one cry.

John Stevens Wade

This time it vanished quite slowly, beginning with the end of the tail, and ending with the grin, which remained some time after the rest of it had gone.

Lewis Carroll

Loves of the cat;
Forgetful even of the rice
Sticking on his whiskers.

Taigi

Why so lean, my lady cat?
Is it fasting causes that?
Say, or is it love?

Matsuo Basho

Sphinx of my quiet hearth! who deignst to dwell
Friend of my toil, companion of mine ease,
Thine is the lore of Ra and Rameses;
That men forget dost thou remember well,
Beholden still in blinking reveries,
With sombre sea-green gaze inscrutable.

Mrs. Tomson

The cat. He walked by himself, and all places were alike to him. He went back through the Wet Wild Woods, waving his wild tail, and walking by his wild lone. But he never told anybody.

Rudyard Kipling

Diamond Cut Diamond

Two cats
One up a tree
One under the tree
The cat up a tree is he
The cat under the tree is she
The tree is witch elm, just incidentally.
He takes no notice of she, she takes no notice of he.
He stares at the woolly clouds passing, she stares at the tree.
There's been a lot written about cats, by old Possum, Yeats and Company
But not Alfred de Musset or Lord Tennyson or Poe or anybody
Wrote about one cat under, and one cat up, a tree.
God knows why this should be left for me
Except I like cats as cats be
Especially one cat up
And one cat under
A witch elm
Tree

Ewart Milne

Cats are not at all like people
        Cats are Cats.

People wear stockings and sweaters,
Overcoats, mufflers, and hats.
Cats wear nothing: they lie by the fire
For twenty-four hours if they desire.
They do NOT rush out to the office,
They do NOT have interminable chats,
They do NOT play Old Maid and Checkers,
They do NOT wear bright yellow spats.

People of course, will always be people,
        But Cats are Cats.

William Jay Smith

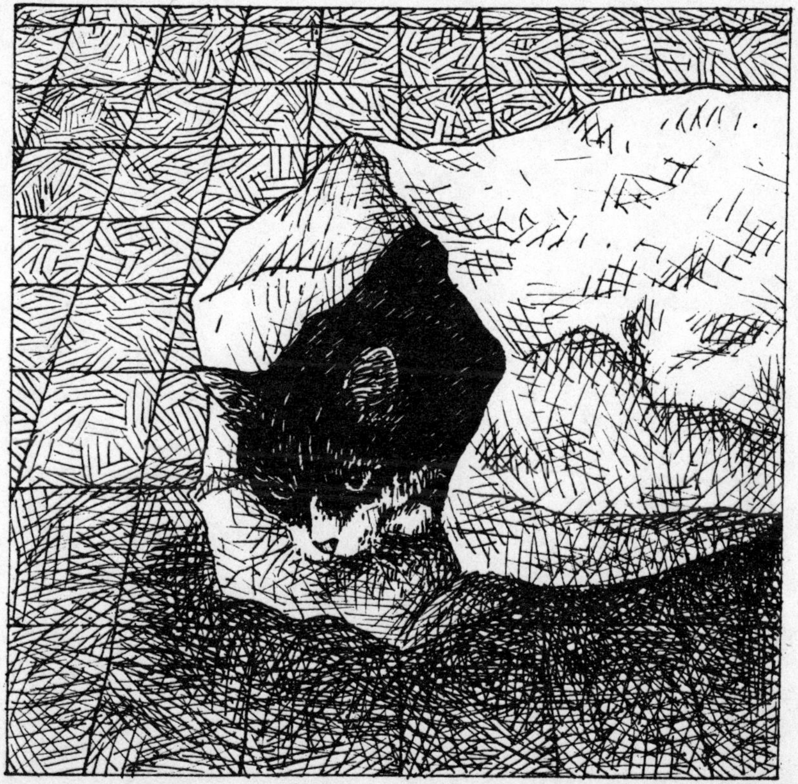

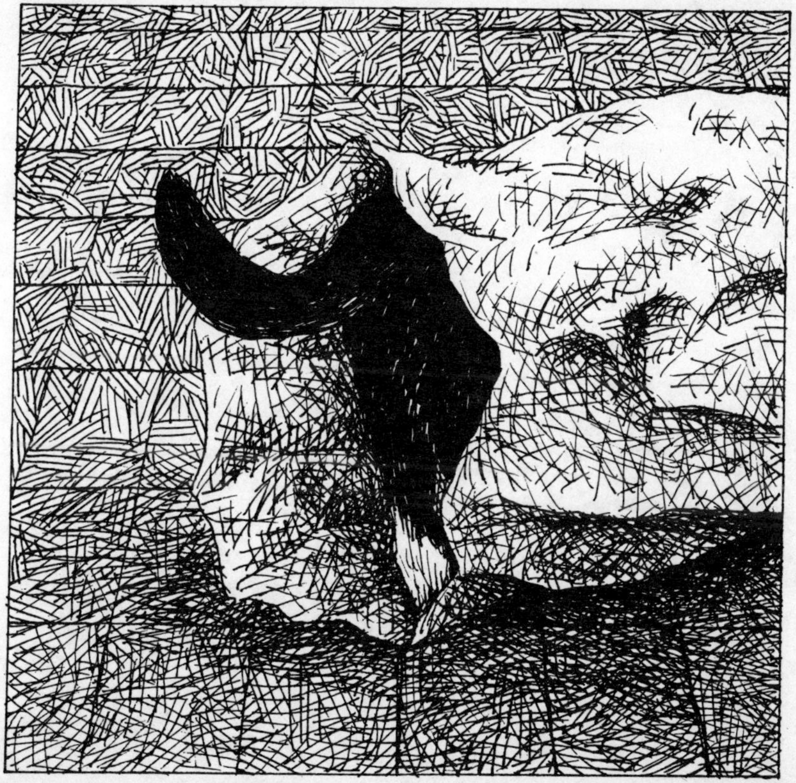